# Why Not LOVE?

by Ken Heitz
Illustrated by Linda Runyon

# Why Not LOVE?

## by Ken Heitz
### Illustrations by Linda Runyon

Published by Linda Runyon's
Wild Food Company
PO Box 83
Shiloh, NJ 08353-0083
lrunyon8@yahoo.com
www.OfTheField.com

**ISBN 0-936699-18-3**

All prose by Ken Heitz
All art by Linda Runyon except as otherwise noted

Layout by Rosary Shepherd
Cover by Eric Conover

For Linda–Your inspiration became my determination--
The key opening the lock of uncertainty

For Eric, Kim & Todd—
for your endurance

and finally for Vicky--thanks B.D.

AVI-70

# Common Ground

Almost 40 years ago during a "BLUE" period in my life while living in an urban environment, I wrote the following verses. Less than a year later the urge to write ended—as did my desire to live the city life.

I now live a secluded, wilderness existence. The effect of my own words was therapeutic enough to influence me to change everything drastically—for the better.

For years people have said my words are inspirational. If so, I want to share them. Maybe you too can change "BLUE" to a more positive attitude.

Ken Heitz

# Introduction

In the early 1970's, Ken and I headed into the woods of the Adirondack Mountains in New York State. Ken's prose came spontaneously, and went on over a period of a year or so. Ken, now my former husband, gave the prose to me.

I just knew a book was in the works. As the years went by, and with God's help, I finally illustrated his prose and *Why Not LOVE?* has become a complete book.

My kudos to my son, Eric Conover, and especially to Rosary Shepherd for the final edit and layouts. A family friend of my daughter, Kevin Street, illustrated the children's section.

*Why Not LOVE?* expresses my thoughts, as well as Ken's. We all hope you feel the same. Enjoy!

Linda Runyon
Illustrator

# Table of Contents

# Why Not Love?

## MY TRUTH

It doesn't matter who I am
        Where I've been
        What I've done.
The following is not justification
        accusation
        vindication.
It just began
        What I see
        and see
        and see. . . .

## LOVE . . . LIGHT . . . LIFE

Love is the way
        mankind can be bound . . .
        Together.
Together is the way
        life can be free.
Free is the way
        Heaven's to be!

# PARADISE LOST?

It is down in man's history
    that we're of the air,
    the land,
    the sea,
    and the tree.
Of all these things
    man can continue
    to be free.
Man's not of the concrete,
    the steel,
    the asphalt,
    the iron.
It's living with these
    the reason we're dying.
For eternity too long
    too many bird songs
    are gone.
Can life any sadder be
    for a boy never to climb a tree,
    smell the salt of the sea?
A paradise lost-
    many cannot remember
    the peace in the valley
    in early September.
Man's thought only of pleasures
    of what he can do,
    not sharing with others
    not even a few.
It's of the air,
    the land,
    the sea,
    and the tree
    that man shall be.

Earth's realness and beauty
         have patiently waited
         yet seem ill fated.
The hope of our world
         lies only in our hands,
         from where do we go
         to find new lands?
Perhaps when man sees
         what really is free,
         he'll let life restore
         what once was before.

# UNIVERSAL LOVE

People are separate entities.
In body,
      but are we in spirit?
We are all guided by
      our emotions,
      and love is an emotion
      within life.
It is love
      that we seek,
      in all that we do.
Much of what we do adds
      to the fire
      of love.
If only we could understand how
      we must direct it,
      and why!
Likened to an infinite flame . . .
      LOVE is the pinnacle
      of life,
      here on earth.
Many have and will experience
      the intensity
      of love.
In this way,
      others feel and understand
      what they cannot explain.
This feeling,
      with self first,
      fellow-man second,
      must be practiced.
When mankind realizes how
      vitally important love is
      to his survival . . .

when he can love
in all that he does,
then will it spread
throughout the world.
As universal love spreads,
it will be recognized.
We all inherently know
what it is.
We seek help
in its kindling
in many ways,
yet drench the flame
out of fear and shame.
We can be set free
as never before.

# LIVING A "TRUTH"

Freedom is shackled
     by humanistic inadequacies—
     a lack of control
     since the beginning,
     has brought thousands
     of years of guilt.
Today's society exists,
     because of basic drives
     to exist.
A turning point
     of existence approaches,
     survival,
     by making reasons
     to exist.
In the understanding
     there exists a reason
     first,
     the seemingly endless progression
     of condition
     is broken.
Understanding is the most positive
     cycle . . .
     towards the truth.
All life was given.
It is the foundation
     of the truth.
The seeds of evolution,
     through time,
     are starting to germinate.
Hope,
     is through this understanding.
Living the truth more,
     will help the progression

towards oneness.
Positivism affords
    the time.
Patience tests the worthiness
    of infinity,
      through positive thought.
Thought is not a positive entity.
The truth is subconsciously
    revealed in fears.
The self,
    being a part,
eliminates the fear
    of loneliness.

Realization of self
    is possible,
    by doing positively,
    for others.
For every action,
    there is a reaction . . .
    infinity.
The real truth is
    a living "truth",
    so that it may continue.
This gives a purpose
    to life.
The games have already begun
    to cease.
Destiny is our choice.
Reality is unquestionably
    justified.
Dreams are becoming
    a reality.
Love is the answer  . . .
    it is the essence of life.

# LOVE HAPPENS

It can't be made,
      altered,
      interfered with,
      destroyed
      or heightened by man.
The sun comes up . . .
      so does love.
You can make it come up in your mind,
      but not really.
Making or
      "faking" love
      is one of man's
      most degrading games -
      to himself.
It must happen -
      minds cannot be forced to meet.
They do—
      but not to have done to them.
      What greater experience
      than to have love happen . . .
      as you live.
You can't live
      to have it happen.
You can't "love to live,"
      you must "live to love."

# PATCHES OF LOVE

The sun smiled a friendly grin
    through dark and looming
    rain-spent clouds of gray,
    shining hope on the remaining day.
The jubilant warmth purveyed
    on storm-drenched soil,
    gave comfort
    to Earth's laborious toil.
Like an eternity indulged
    in worry and grief,
    came the sun's welcome relief.
Patches of brightness
    laid down from above,
    like a huge quilt blanket,
    stitched by heaven's hands of love.
Threatening shadows
    of darkness and gloom,
    breaking and fading
    so flowers may bloom.
From eyes smoked and teary,
    A face that's so sad,
    to visions seen clearly
    for hearts now
    are glad.

# WHO IS MAN?

Scientific,
        logical
        reasoning man . . .
"There is an answer for everything."
        Yes, of course.
Why then the diversion
        from the most basic question of all?
        Why is man's existence possible?
Why is it even there?
        To continue man's investigation. . . .
        Yes . . . but for what reason?
For the promotion of man's imaginary
        into reality dreams?
Is that the only reason
        to continue man's existence?
Or, is man using only a portion
        of his potential level,
        diverting it only to
        what will make his existence easier,
        as he sees it?
His advancements are,
        no doubt,
        nothing short of spectacular.
What then the creation
        of the very laboratory he lives in,
        his world?
Are not the existing creations around him,
        the air,
        sky,
        waters,
        trees,
        animals,
        his fellow man,

just that spectacular?
Or are they just taken for granted?
How do we see them?
Obtaining everything that is a result
of man's materialistic imagination?
What do you have . . .
When you have it all?
How do you obtain happiness?
Do you work for it?
Do you obtain the very thing
man lives and strives for,
through "success and prosperity?"
Or do you only think you do?
Of course it's relative—
But isn't it only relative
along the same line of thinking?
Is man willing to admit that
PEACE—
HAPPINESS cannot be purchased?
For GOD's sake,
why does man alienate himself
from the very necessities he wants,
by continuing a way of life
that can undermine that which he seeks?

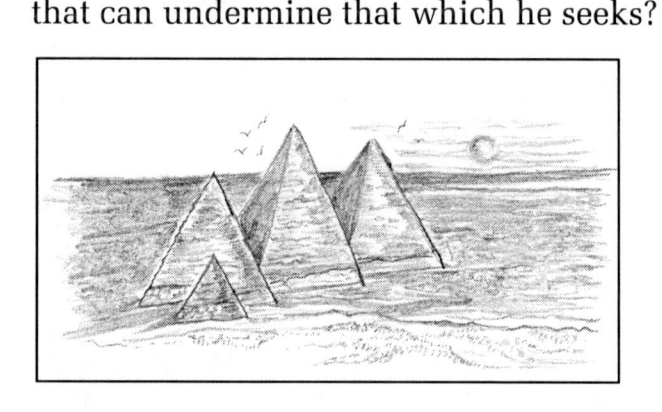

# CHRIST WAS A MAN

Long, long ago
    far across the sea
    a man named Christ
    came to be.
Christ was a man
    like you and me.
A super man
    with super pride
    spread broad and wide,
    for all to see.
His pride was not
    of country or land,
    but of all His fellow man.
A man with wisdom . . .
    a man who knew
    what men must do
    and why.
Christ's words were spoken,
    heard then and now,
His heart was broken,
    deaf ears words could not pierce.
But He said then
    He'd return someday,

but said then
which way.
Had then been today . . .
had He said today
He'd be back someday,
what words would be spoken
for the countless more hearts
broken.
Christ was a man,
like you and me.
He had said what He could
to help man see.
What Christ had to say
could show the way,
if understood yesterday.
In your hearts,
be His words. . . .
Understand and live then
today
as you understand today
your way.
Christ said He'd return
someday
to save tomorrow.

# AWARENESS

Awareness is recognition
      of existence—
Awareness is a level,
      providing the "source
      of light *to see*,"
      providing a world
      in which *to exist*.
Through awareness,
      man strengthens himself,
      through the acquisition
      of knowledge.
The extent of knowledge is
      limited to one's level
      of awareness.
Where the light fades
      so does the sight.
We are a level
      of awareness—
Now as a race . . .
      the human race—
      upon this planet.
We are the highest known
      form of intelligence
      upon this earth.
We are now at a level
      of existence and knowledge,
      whereby, we are aware
our process of thought is
      in a form of
      energy—
We are attaining a level
      of energy,
      to which we NOW are

of a ONENESS—
a single force,
The truth is within
all of us,
for we are all
within it—
The truth is
the first step
toward eventual
freedom!

# THE HEAD OF MAN

The masses—
    the establishment,
    the educated,
    the educators—
These are the leaders of society—
    of the world.
They are the ones
    who have brought civilization
    to what it is. . . .
They are the thinkers,
    the inventors,
    the creators of technological marvels.
How can such brilliance of intelligence
    come from such narrow-minded
    "one-way" thinkers?
Do they leave any choice?
    Is not theirs the only way?
    By numbers alone,
    theirs becomes the only way . . .
    "To live."
By their designation,
    "white is white—
    black is black."
They say all has been done
    and is being done for man . . .
That leaves very little for questioning.
    Just ask them.
    How about yourself?
What is man's life and reasons
    for existence all about?
Is it "success?"
    Basically, but what?
Prosperity?

Wealth?
Obtaining everything that is a result
Perhaps because man hasn't
created - *anything* - everything,
he constantly struggles to
out-do that which he has not done!!
Why not stop in wonderment
of these marvels . . .
and appreciate . . .
not ignore, with the attitude of
"So what, look at what we have done."
Just look at what we've done. . . .
Could any of it have been done
without the one unequaled masterpiece
of our all time,
time itself?
What happens the very moment
the "spark of life" comes to the newborn?
Does he grow and "mature"
to a useful citizen of society?
Unquestionably, not always.
We say "some make it, some don't."
But who has set up the yardstick?
Is it not possible for a child
to grow to almost any form
of society?
He does just that
all around the world,
in many and varied ways.
But, it all,
no matter what societies or
philosophies of life,
starts the same way.
In that respect,
all mankind is created equal.

# TIME FOR THE NEW MAN

The face of the earth
      can be likened to that of man -
      in need of change -
      time to put forth
      a new image of man.
Change is underway -
      that of unification.
Unification of belief in values,
      Life . . .
      existence.
This belief must be supported
      through "living" one's belief.
Talk is not enough.
      People will not accept
      nor understand
      what has not been done -
It must be related to in "reality."
Living as you believe
      the way man was intended,
      instructed,
      created,
      is the only way universal happiness,
      understanding,
      brotherhood -
      will come about.
Peace and understanding
      will promote the same
      to others.
A smile will eliminate a frown -
      warmth will pierce the chill.
The word must be spread.
      Pure,
      real,

"faithful" exposure of emotion
cannot and will not be stopped.
Live it -
be it -
it is what you want . . .
for you,
me,
for all . . . and it will.

# TRUTH EQUALS LIFE

The very essence of life
    is recognized by feeling,
    or emotion.
Whatever is done . . .
    in work or play,
    existence is realized by
    one guideline . . .
    the truth!
Knowledge is the truth,
    through understanding.
What is understanding?
    Helping others to be knowledgeable
    of themselves.
The smallest variation
    from truth,
    is dishonesty,
    inflicting guilt and
    the emotion fear,
    propagating more guilt . . .
    more fear.
This negative cycle associates
    the admission of guilt
    with punishment!!
To avoid this,
    and preserve the self,
    from fear,
    we lie . . .
    further guilt.
The negative chain continues.
By not wanting to cope
    with a world of guilt,
    for lack of truth,

We have produced an
UNDERSTANDING GAP!

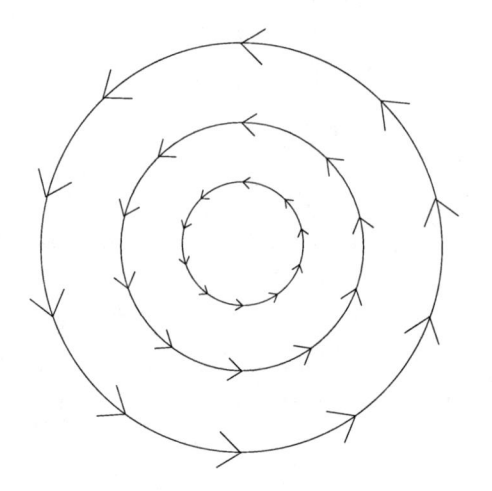

## LOVE IS

Love is like a gentle morn
      the light of life
      just freshly born.
Love is like petals
      of pastel splendor
      pink and white,
      yellow and lavender.
Love is like a bright blue sky,
      a blanket of peace
      far as the eye can see.
Love is like the tallest mountain,
      the highest high
      that can be.
Love is like a gentleman
      in whose presence
      you're warm inside.
A man whose heart
      he does not hide.
Love is like all there can be,
      for you are you
      and
      I am me!

# LOVE

The eternal tides,
     rolling waves of endurance,
     ascending and falling
     like leaves of a tree,
     budding and departing
     to tempos that ring free
     of distraction.
The presence of love
     floating freely
     on calm winds of trust,
     like the essence of a fall forest
     judged not by color, nor worth or stature,
     cowering not to the fear of itself.
For love is not conquered,
     no enemies do challenge,
     love seeks not repentance
     for rewards long forgotten.
Love's time is not measured
     by moments to be,
     love's foundation is man
     to freely be given.
Love chooses not to be silent,
     wishes only to remain,
     counts not numbered rainbows,
     love shines not of lust.
Love sees not of man
     what he should see,
     man is of her tender,
     love's heart is a guide,
     a trinket of oneness,
     for love does not hide.

# PLANNED?

What is life
      and its many and varied facets,
      but a program.
A program constantly being updated,
      as its demands change,
      whether it be good or bad.
Everything about man -
      ALL is guided,
      ruled,
      helped,
      hindered
      as a result of a program.
Is it the only one
      by which man,
      as he sees himself,
      can function?
Is it wrong to question the program?
      No!
If you feel the program
      needs modification,
      what do you do?
Do you scrap the whole program . . .
      Do you escape?
That is to say,
      do you cease to exist,
      which does absolutely nothing?!
What is a program?
      Supposedly a logical set of rules
      governing logical chains of commands
      and events.
Good!! But what is logic?
      For that matter,

what is anything?
        Isn't it all an extension of man . . .
Part of one giant program by which
        man CAN exist?
What or where did it start?
        Why did it begin -
        awareness,
        thought,
        questioning,
        answers. . .
        *anything*?
Man may and has tried to
        clinically answer the physical
        existence of most of it . . .
        or has he?
Is it all coincidence . . .
        a scientific chain of events?
Scientifically answer why
        man can THINK
        and for what reason.

# WHERE DID IT ALL BEGIN?

It really doesn't matter . . .
       this is not ours to deal with.
What about where it ends?
       There will be no end to love . . .
       this way -
       this time.
Ours is but to
       "aid" in its functions.
To be as tools in its creation.
       Everything necessary
       to help it evolve is there,
       and always has been.
We have not wanted to see it,
       for infinite reasons . . .
       but it is inevitable
       If its very "life-giving" strength
       is to SURVIVE.
No one has,
       can,
       or will be able to say they haven't seen
       it.
They will . . .
       as the struggle increases,
       the answer becomes brighter -
       then they will see.
It must begin with one's self.
       Only there can it be understood.
It can't be taught
       as we know teaching—
Or learned
       as we know learning.
It will be known,
       as you and only you know

YOU must be.
You will try to define,
  categorize,
  and clarify it to yourself
  to no avail.
It can only be -
  as it is to you.
You will know,
  by your life,
  why and how it must be . . .
  UNIVERSALLY.

## THE SELF

The self—
        seems the most important
        thing you must protect
        from pain.
This is called
        self-preservation.
But,
        what is the use
        of preserving only
        the self—
        if nothing else is to be
        preserved?
Without others—
        everyone seems to be
        reverting to individual worlds,
        together - yet apart,
        together - yet lonely.
The self is to be mutually
        shared,
        respected,
        trusted,
        among all of us.

# TO COMPLETE ONESELF

Now, we all know
      you only reap
      what you sow -
With the passing of time
      from long, long ago
      one's wish to ease the soul
      remains so.
It may have been the wheel
      that's made what is real.
Man's need to love . . .
      man's need to feel,
      cannot be man-made.
We can make ourselves
      feel our love of life,
      or of the wheel.
One's wish to ease the soul
      may bring the day
      no one will feel
      tomorrow.
It may not be
      in your day,
      for the wheel came
      not yesterday,
But from then till now,
      we have all forgotten
      how to live,
      to love . . .
We knew not then
      how today would be . . .
We can look back
      how we've changed,
      how aware we are. . . .

Let us not forget that
      consciousness of all that man's done
      is incomplete
      without appreciation
      of man himself. . . .
Life with all man's exploration
      cannot complete
      the most basic feat
      to complete oneself.

# MYSELF

Yes,
       I can know myself too well,
       sometimes,
       not knowing too much,
       but knowing till not sure
       how it all fits at all times.
       "Human first!"
Well,
       I see what I want to see,
       it can't stop there—
I see it as I would like it,
       as I know it could be,
       but also know
       it might not be.
It is here that I wonder
       if I have it right,
       or, if it has me wrong.
Should I believe
       all that I think will happen?
Should I dismiss
       all that I am not sure will happen?
Should I try
       to make it happen
       as I see it?
I feel that it won't happen
       if I'm in doubt,
       or, will doubt
       make it not happen?
This relationship to my head
       is only to me.
If it involves another's head,
       it becomes infinitely open
       to confusion,

as to fact versus cold fact.
Fact—You are you,
     I am me . . .
I can't be you,
     nor you me . . .
But we can share it all.
Is it all worth it?
     or is only me too much
     as it is?
No, this is life,
     in its most basic,
     yet encompassing form.
If these doubts and confusions
     can't be dealt with,
     or even lived with,
     then one cannot claim
     to be able to live at all.
To me, it is as necessary
     as the sun itself.

## "TICK-TOCK"

Peace of mind -
      "being"
      "alive"
   is making time me
Not having time pass by -
    watching it . . .
What is time,
    but my head?
When my head isn't "right on"
    time becomes perceptively different—
    an object of tangibility.
Usually a threat . . .
    But, when my head is me
    I make time!
      "making"—
      "using"—
Not being carried,
    altered,
    being used . . .
"TICK - TOCK?"
    Not really—
"To-Be!" ME!!

## LIFE

What is the program
        of life?
A program constantly being
        updated,
        demands change.
Everything is a result
        of the program?
The program of Earth is
        a cycle of causes
        and events,
        part of a larger program,
        limited to the boundaries
        of infinity.
Is it all coincidence
        that man can think?

# COMPASSION

There are infinite "why's",
     "when's",
     and "wherefore's".
This is more of the same reasoning,
     because of a natural desire
     to know,
     to comprehend. . . .
The more facts and figures,
     the more distant the necessary.
Mankind could do nothing
     but THINK
     forever . . .
     provided there will BE forever.
Given a start,
     a jump on the pace
     of evolution,
     is indicative of a platform
     of compassion.
Civilization on Earth today,
     advanced sociologically
     and scientifically
     infiltrate and exploit,
     and perish.
The moral guidelines passed on
     have led to
     an understanding
     of something a great deal
     more important to existence . . .
     UNIVERSAL PEACE!

## FEELING

May we soon see
      that we have in fact,
      only replaced,
      through extensions of ourselves . . .
      the car for walking,
      the boat for swimming,
      the plane for flying,
      and now,
      the computer for thinking!
All replaced in an effort to *gain*
      the very thing that makes us
      differ from the rest
      of nature,
      the ability to consciously *feel*,
      to love,
      to relate,
      emotionally, through our ability
      to think.

# THE CYCLE

It's all here -
       in balance.
A cycle
       Providing all life
       necessary.
We are all part of rhythmatic harmony.
Nature thinks not
       of supplementation,
       betterment,
       briefing.
Life is a multicolored,
       perpetual wave of energy
       of gyrating complexity.
Though mass and energy
       are theoretically conserved
       the ratio of balance within
       limits of time (is in direct proportion)
       to its respective need!
The macro-organism of thought,
       dependent on life for supplementation,
       stands in reflection
       of the scales so determining
       its conclusion.

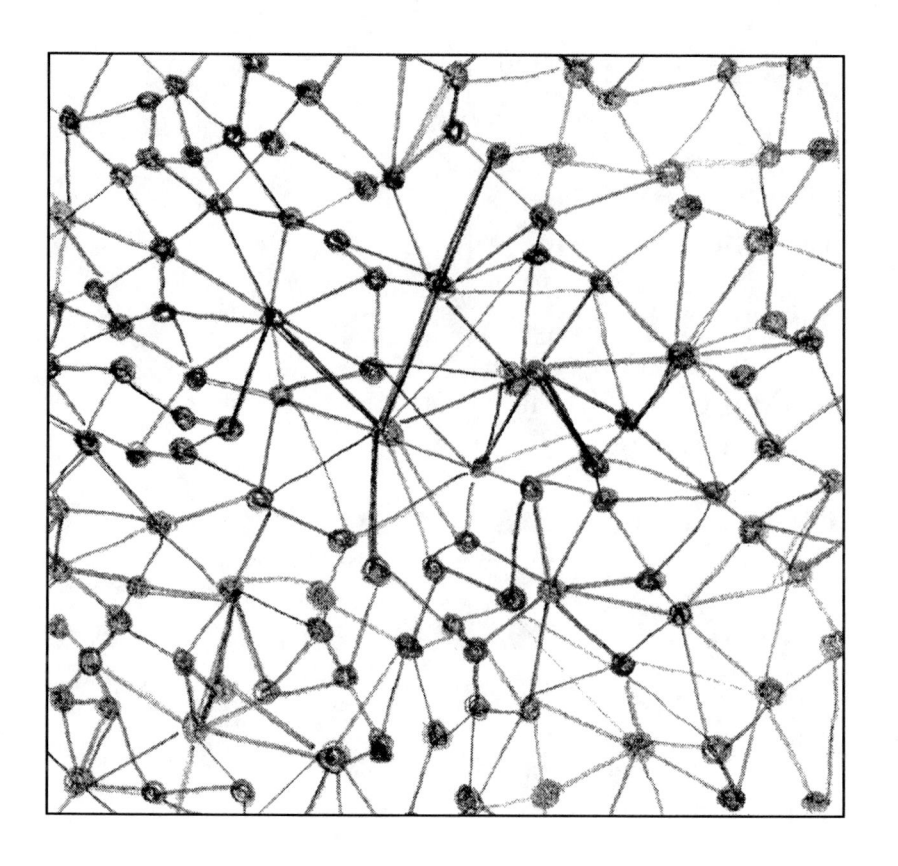

# CIRCLE OF INFINITY

Is there another world,
     other than what is "seen"?
It is called
     the subconscious.
But,
     what is its purpose?
Could it be another level
     of awareness?
Can we relate
     dreaming
     to what we subconsciously think
     awake?
Do we "exist,
     therefore we are aware?"
Or,
     "We are aware,
     therefore we exist?"

# THE PAST

The past is a relation
     of time,
     to the present—
     through accumulating events
     that have bridged a gap from
     "then to now."
Positive thinking can only
     make the future.
No matter what the objective,
     it cannot be obtained . . .
     without "positivism."
Nothing exists,
     that doesn't exist
     in your mind.
You must control it,
     though often it is
     controlled.
No one person has
     created it all—
But, everyone can know what exists.
Without the clock,
     would time exist at all?

# FUTURE MEMORIES

Yesterdays unfold aplenty,
    standing edge to edge,
    linking the haze of infinity with today.
Memories in disguise,
    like white birch
    in a snowy forest,
    linger and lace moments ago,
    till alerted.
Dark hallways and dusty closet shelves,
    laden with aged remnants,
    appear and fade without warning,
    of times long forgotten.
Blind trail blazing ahead,
    outruns only freedom,
    for today rests but lightly
    and shortly will pass,
    becoming shy of future,
    a memory at last.

# CONSCIOUSNESS

Consciousness is a dream
       of existence
       visual proof
       of reality.
To step in time
       and see it all again,
       to be it all again,
       is the same consciousness,
       the same dream
       relived—
       again.
The fearless energy
       of time
       in your mind
       conserves consciousness
       through the balance
       of past and future,
       fear and love.
Everyone knows their
       thoughts,
       when time is taken
       to examine the relationship
       between thoughts,
       a conscious addition
       surfaces!

# MAKE TIME FREE

Step by step—
       from then till now,
       past is past,

now is now.
Past was present—
    now is future to then.
Future will always be
    tomorrow . . .
Past will always be yesterday—
What then will be today?
Yesterdays are many . . .
    many are mistakes.
Yet,
    yesterdays are past,
    and the past is gone.
Soon today will be past
    and gone.
Will today be a mistake?
Will tomorrow reflect
    what today was not?
Only yesterdays
        add up to today.
Let's make a new start . . .
    a new day.
Free today of yesterdays!
Make today . . .
    TODAY!

## THEN & NOW

Is there a man
        because of his color
        who can share his life . . .
        all love and strife . . .
        so I can see
        why he must be,
        what he must.
It's not the color
        that shines in my eyes
        it's his thoughts
        it's his feelings
        it's the man I can see—
If this man knew
        how I see,
This man would know how
        he wants to be
        with me.
For in the end,
        the beginning again;
We all shall know—
        it's in between
        then and now
        that we must learn
        how!

# EQUALITY

So true
>      is the phrase
>      "all men are created equal."
We are born flesh and blood
>      and molded within
>      our capabilities.
We are born human beings
>      first . . .
Some are weak . . .
>      some strong . . .
>      some talented . . .
>      some not—
But,
>      these are manifestations
>      of our society,
>      making the individual
>      a part of the whole.
Do we accept ourselves
>      individually,
>      or, submit our free will
>      to a ruling minority?

# TIME

Time is an industrious craftsman . . .
        ever creating,
        ever lasting,
        freeing itself with never ending change
        to its face . . .
        never really angry,
        never sad.
A dazzling display
        of zig-zagging rays of light
        cut through an early morning mist,
        and a new day had begun.
The air is still
        and warm.
A busy squirrel
        darts among the logs
        of the woodpile,
        breakfasting on an array
        of nuts.
The shells splintered and cracked
        lay scattered about.
An owl,
        perched aloft
        in a nearby tree,
        provides a song to accompany
        the morning's light show
        of color and sound.
A small mouth bass,
        cracks the water's skin
        in the lake below.
Here life is wonder all around.
In time with itself . . .

Giving of itself
　　　　as only its balance
　　　　could always remain.
A new day
　　　　and yet really just
　　　　yesterday's
　　　　end!!

# POSITIVE - NEGATIVE

Peace - tranquility
    of the mind
    is as enigmatic
    to deal with as is
    turmoil - despair!
The mind has long associated
    with confused . . .
Peace cannot be understood
    in respect to anything
    the mind has experienced.
Recognition of this fact alone
    will help solidify peace
    with its proper respect
    to existence.
Knowledge of what peace
    is not . . .
    will aid in keeping
    it under control.
Not letting negative forces
    create a false illusion
    of loss of mind.
Confusion - - - - - - - Peace
One must find the point,
    along infinity
    that can be kept -
    progression towards greater peace
    will come slowly
    as the mind adjusts
    to any point.
Losing the foothold
    you exist in,
    is worse than never having

come there at all.
Losing tranquility
      is worse than never having it.
The higher you go -
      the harder you can fall.
You will catch
      your descent
      and return higher
      than before
      with greater understanding.
The positive forces
      of love and trust
      is the strongest rope
      offered to you.
Starting with self,
      as in reflection of God -
      the control and strength offered
      to you
      for a purpose -
      YOUR purpose.
Find out first -
      where you are,
      before you begin.
You cannot walk blindly.
      Lead yourself
      to where you want to be.

## TRUST OF SELF

There she is -
      she's almost sure.
She wants to be,
      for it's the cure.
It's trust she needs
      from you and me.
But it's okay
      someday -
She will know
      which way to go.
It's trust she needs
      to understand.
It may seem far -
      but really close at hand . . .
The only help
      through all the rest
      cannot be given,
      it must be found.
Trust of self is
      by far the best!

# I AM

I love you
    to love me.
Will I return
    your love
    with love of myself?
I trust you
    because,
    you trust me.
May I trust myself?
Without you,
    there is no need
    for me.

# THE REASONS WHY

We, the able,
  of Mind, Body, and Spirit,
  have the fortune of offering
  a hand to those who -
  through the waning
  of their years -
  need our assistance.
We can ease
  the troubled,
  assist the ill.
We have,
  through the years,
  learned and will continue
  to learn how
  we can help
  one in need.
Age may have taken
  its toll
  of the body,
But,
  the spirit is always
  willing.
We understand how
  we can help another
  our elders,
  understand the greatest prescription
  on earth,
  to care . . .
The everyday miracle!

# THE OLD

The old -
      our stepping stones
      to the now,
Are to be respected,
      honored,
      and given a helping hand
      from us,
      their pathway to the future.
From the young
      to the old -
      passing their years
      to their young.
And from the young
      to the old -
The cycle of life.
May we be honored
      to do our part now -
      for them.

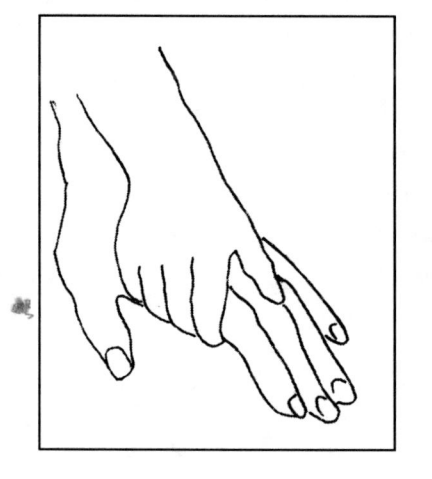

# WHAT'S GOING ON?

Look at what is going on
        around us.
We all presently share
        our surroundings . . .
        EARTH.
What are we doing
        as a race?
A great deal is being done,
        both good and wrong,
        by all of us.
What can we do
        to better the situation?
Many people think,
        regardless of present circumstances,
        if something is done wrong,
        it will be corrected
        at a later date.
The significance of
        "a later date"
        takes for granted a point
        would not be reached,
        where we don't have further time
        for corrective measure.
As human beings,
        we are all subject to influences,
        we may not consciously accept.
Cause and effect
        is constant . . .
        it never stops.
For every action,
        there is a reaction,
        both literal and psychological.

If effect is unique to our own
      conscious personality,
      each individual,
      based on conditioning,
      has his own line of existence.
This line is total of all previous,
      present, and future conditioning.
If nothing were to change,
      then the present would never
      change.
Right now would be
      the rest of time.
Perhaps everything that brings
      pain and confusion,
      will be controlled
      someday.
How about death?
Maybe modern science
      will solve that too . . .
      but, at what price?
Change is always present.
People make change
Recognizing changes
      gives the ability
      to control the effects.
This could be called . . .
      UNDERSTANDING . . .
      the cause and effect
      psychological relationships
      between influences of change
      and ourselves.

# PASSAGE OF TIME

The passage of time
    is like falling snow . . .
    elusive,
    yet in constant motion,
    swirling and tumbling
    to its crystalline bed below,
    only to return to
    the heights above
    with the glowing sun.
A motionless tree
    towering above,
    like a balloon above its cord,
    is masked white.
Like a fence post,
    painted by the wind and snow,
    ridged arms in all directions,
    drooping under the weight
    of the world.
Time floats by
    with each whispering flake.
Footprints trail off endlessly,
    depressing the frozen cloud
    upon the ground.
To the rear,
    the valleys sculptured
    by heavy boots,
    are smoothed and covered
    like a brook
    covering its basin,
    and the passage of time
    is erased.

One more step
    and the wheels and cogs
    of heaven's time
    set in motion again.
Time is as free as
    the drifting, bleached gems
    of ice.
Free as the billows of air
    moving about.
The light gleams instantly
    on frozen snow,
    blaring and blinding,
    like a motion picture screen
    of intensity,
    cupping your eyes
    with a dazzling energy.

Crystalline rocks of ice
     jet downward,
     piercing the skin
     of reality,
     just to say hello
     against a background
     of negative black.
The jutting structures
     barely able to cast a shadow,
     angled and bent
     by the orbiting sun,
     come alive
     and grow,
     to the sun's relief.
Drip,
     then another,
     timed only by light rays
     well penetrated,
     reflected and refracted,
     combined and apart.
Drops of perfection,
     aimed at Earth's heart,
     fired back to point
     of origin,
     and loved,
     like mother for child.
From start to end
     only forever ends not
     but to start again!

# DEATH

Death may be
    an experience of what life was
    to us,
    and what it might
    have been . . .
The past and the future
    locked without time
    and the presence
    of death
    is what was told man
    will be for us
    eternally!!!

# HOPE

There is hope . . .
    hope of all hope,
    that life will culminate
    to be what it must,
    to prepare for
    the next step.
Such a long time -
    such a long need -
    ever present
    never fully understood
    just what was
    to be.
Hope is flourishing -
    for man to find
    a way -
    to realize where
    he is heading
    and why.

Through God,
   man has been making
   it happen,
   but he hasn't really seen,
   really known,
   he will,
   for he knows
   he must,
   from delusion . . .
   to INFINITY!

# EYES

Eyes are for seeing,
  yet what can be seen?
The eyes are only external sight . . .
  or is it just an illusion?
We can cloud the sight
  and paint a different scene.
Yet,
   doesn't it still exist?
Does a cloud,
  blanketing a forest
  remove the trees?
Is the real picture
  repaintable—
  can't the fog be lifted?
When the fog is lifted,
  is the picture the same . . .
  for all?
No thing in reality
  is the same,
  externally or internally.
Faith in yourself,
  in the sense that
  no one else sees it
  EXACTLY that way,
  reveals the soul.

# THE LIVING WINDOWS

Through panes of glass,
     some sparkling like still waters,
     some stained of distorted impressions,
     come pictures,
     alive . . .
Some worth sure of admiration,
     some like the feel of freedom,
     painted with colors careless
     with irresponsible deed,
     imagery unstylist.
Portholes, aware not of deception,
     lucent pathways of truth . . .
One hallway of sight,
     most important of all,
     opens not to worlds without,
     it hangs on the wall,
     sees what others do
     without a doubt.

# SOUND

Let your ears be your eyes
    and behold the colors of sound
    around you.
Listen to the tempo of a gurgling brook,
    smoothing and polishing
    multi-colored stones,
    journeying to a distant lake
    that glimmers like gold.
The eddies and swirls of a miniature fall
    caress the air
    with crystal clear notes.
Bubbling and brimming,
    like a whisper to mountains above
    of its cleanliness.
Hear the soft whistles
    of sturdy pines
    breathing a gentle wind
    like a sigh of gratitude
    for the breath of life.
A field of wild wheat,
    golden brown from the sun,
    sings to blue skies above,
    waving hands to the heavens
    and speaking in graceful delight.
A symphony of voices
    heard all over the Earth,
    no one need see them
    to know of their worth!

# SAND AND SEA

Froth and foam
    of the boiling salty brine,
    caresses the face of sandy shore,
    and melts into a tidal surge.
Endlessly,
    a procession of watery walls,
    rolling and crumbling
    like the last,
    cascades a mountain of aqueous spill,
    with essence,
    and gusto.
The resonant thrill is
    the rhythmic cadence,
    in concert to the sun and moon.
Sea and sand embracing
    with a cradle of tan,
    combing a perfect union.
The marriage of worlds,
    their numbers are three,
    exists in a paradise of heaven
    for you
    and for me.

# DAY BY NIGHT

The midnight ball of light
    passes over the waves,
    like a revealing sight.
The languor of time
    from a sliver at water's crest,
    to a looming presence above,
    is a time of peacefulness,
    drifting upward
    like the leisure of understanding.
A shower of white
    from a rumbling swell's peak,
    bursts forth through
    the moon-bathed night sea
    like a rain of glowing mist.
Out of the flowing land
    a gull circles,
    appearing and dissolving,
    with whisper clouds
    shading the incandescent sphere.
Even through the still of night,
    there survives the presence of light.
The luminescence of dawn's
    sculptured awareness,
    'til eventide's muted sheen.
A loyal luster helps life clean
    what is not.
Its lights shimmering attendance
    that life may make acquaintance.

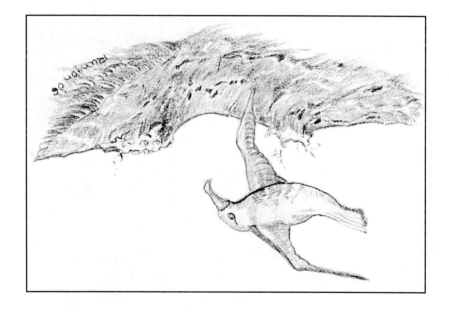

# SPREADING WARMTH

In the depths of night
    a faint orange glow appears
    far in the distance.
Pencils of light beams mix together
    in spectacular fashion
    to help the horizon.
For endless moments,
    the sun's rim of brilliance
    emerges from the edge of two worlds,
    where sky and sea are one.
Like a radiant companion
    of warmth and love,
    the sun's cordial presence
    gives of itself,
    a mind full of life,
    for all life to see.
The earthbound creations
    of nature's combining,
    a balance of activity,
    of frolic and fun,
    where all Earth's existence
    but man
    stand as one.

# HARMONY

Take a look slowly . . .
    before you lay wonders
    abound,
    chiseled beauty,
    honed perfection,
    polished and bright.
A daybreak blinks
    gray hued statues,
    molded with grace,
    garnished gaily
    with the essence of love
    in tribute to the four winds.
An engulfing panoramic composite
    of harmony,
    finely balanced and tuned,
    created and recreating
    a perpetual peace.
Challenging the approaching dusk
    of orange and gold,
    crests of earth,
    like statues in bronze,
    shade the horizon
    to tell their worth.
Slipping silently
    into berths of darkness,
    sleeping with the peace
    of an inviting pine breeze.
Lowering their shades
    one by one,
    till only a trace of sweetness
    remains!

# WINGS OF LOVE

With a gentle motion,
     a mourning dove brushed
     her feathered wings
     against the mountain air.
Just enough as if to whisper
     "thank you"
     to her companion in flight
     the wind,
     and touched down,
     with a graceful bound,
     upon an evergreen brightly sprinkled
     with an early mist.
The air is fresh
     the sky intensely clear hue.
Imagine the dove's pleasure
     while gliding about his sea
     of blue.
Let's try to fly
     for it is our sky, too!
Let your thoughts drift
     upon the wings of our friend,
     the dove.
With a hearty leap from our perch
     and with a thrust
     of feather carpeted arms,
     we take to the heavens.
Climbing swiftly upward,
     our hearts become our guide.
The smell of the forest,
     like the honey of unjaded pine,
     whisks by us
     as we clear the tallest trees,
     limbs reaching for the sun.

See the stream's
      sparkling smile below,
      reflections of light bubble and break
      like a million tiny mirror flakes
      rippled by the breeze.
A carpet of green and brown
      sleeps peacefully
      as far as you can see.
Earth's gift of wonderment
      to you.
You circle a mountain's edge,
      banking, climbing,
      swooping, diving.
A breathless flight
      of love,
Love of all you see . . .
      all you feel.
What gift is more real?

A flock of mallard
    seem to float effortlessly
    along with you,
    on their way to a summer's rest.
The bracing air whistles by your ears -
    you feel no fears.
This treat is too fine
    to let anything steal your mind.
A sloping hillside
    that seems to tilt the Earth
    moves slowly along
    as though pushed by the hands
    of heaven.
Could it be you are not moving at all?
It's such a pretty scene
    it doesn't matter.
For it is appreciation
    that allows you to love.
A forest of pine wisps upward from below,
    like tiny green springs of life
    pointing to the stars saying "Hello."
Our dove is descending earthward now
    past the emerald quills . . .
Our nostrils are filled with the scent
    of nature's perfume
    and on a bed of fluffy moss
    we feather lightly down.
Such a splendid journey
    claims no reward.
We may go again -  anytime.

# TRUTH

May we thank God
      for our ability to see
      in others,
      that which we see
      in ourselves -
      love,
      trust,
      and understanding.
Seeing as He sees us -
      belief in others -
      as He believes in us -
      our search for His Truth
      not an extension
      of our own.
There is but one Truth,
      one guideline for which
      we set up our humanistic
      yardsticks to guide us.
We know what is right -
      and what we've made
      to be right.
God!
      Give us the "feeling" to give
      thanks to You,
      for us,
      for it all.
It all will culminate to be
      what He wills.
May we have the strength
      to aide in its growth -
We've been helped
      this far,
      may we finish

what began -
Understanding and love
of all mankind,
as He does us!

# THE CHILDREN

Look at the children
     of all races,
     colors,
     nationalities.
What do you see?
Listen to their joy
     and laughter -
Children imitate adults,
     so why does the smile fade
     so quickly?
Why does the laughter stifle?
Does their "education"
     represent real love
     and honesty?
Children offer the chance
     to make a world
     of peace and happiness!
Listen -
     as they thank us -
     for the example we give
     them. . . .


# CHILDREN OF LIFE

To the children of life
     on which life's love has shone
May you be happy
     in all that you do . . .
May you cherish your gifts
     of life,

in the spirit
in which they were given . . .
My you feel the trueness
of love,
of yourselves,
of each other -
May you always face
each dawn with
understanding -
for no greater gift
can be obtained
than to want for another
what joys you possess.
God has blessed you
with life
in His image . . .
May we all share
His gift
forever.

# MATURITY

It's a relation of maturity,
  that is, a vital key to success
  of a master plan.
Experience,
  whether good or bad,
  to uplifted awareness,
  has to be carefully considered.
It is important to
  obviate a few who will have the control
  "to use," through understanding -
  than to excite the masses of those
  not as stimulated through time.
They will be more motivated by
  "their" relation to those
  whom they know -
  for those that they do, in fact,
  hold some respect.
Let us not lose sight
  of the fact, that
  there are many who are *ready* -
  educationally,
  sociologically,
  and spiritually . . .
Look at us . . . Why now?  Not earlier?
WE have attained
  that which is necessary
  to propagate such a
  magnanimous task—
WE MUST teach
  other teachers first.

## PURPOSE

We all have a job to do . . .
>    it's in "payment," if you will,
>    for our entire being.

Such a challenge -
>    never ending.

Sometimes distressing,
>    but the rewards -
>    HUMANITY itself.

You can never be nowhere again.
It's you . . .
>    Me . . .
>    love.

ALL TOTAL,
>    consuming in infinite purity
>    and understanding.

You know what must be . . .
>    Total and absolute justification
>    for *all* existence.

## TO BE

Far as we can go . . .
Far as we can see  . . .
There are infinite ways
       to be.
Our center of thought
       is where we are,
         not where we could be.
Limited places,
       to center our thought,
         free will at our command . . .
We are not alone.
Learning all the time,
       we make time.
It is up to us
       to have today . . .
It is up to us
       to have TOMORROW!

# LOVE=LIGHT=LOVE=LIFE

Life is the means
       by which love can be found.
To mankind to which
       we are bound,
       can we live life
       can we understand
       what we do not?
In life's understanding
       may we appreciate love
       of which we are a part.
In love's light
       we are able to see life
       in love's understanding . . .
May we continue to do so
       FOREVER!

# About the Author

Ken Heitz was born in 1946 in Pennsylvania. After school, he served in the Coast Guard and eventually went to work for IBM as a field engineer. When he met Linda Runyon he was at his wit's end from a divorce, the result being the loss of his two small children and his job.

Mired in despair, Ken abruptly started hearing words in his mind. He began writing them down. He wrote only for himself- they were not intended for anyone else. It was cathartic. The words flowed for about a year. Ken says, "It was either that, or the top of my head would have blown off."

He eventually showed some poems to Linda Runyon, the illustrator of this book, and she was quite taken with them.

After Ken and Linda were married, they visited the Adirondack Mountains of upstate New York and decided to move there. Inspired, they went back home and sold everything. They homesteaded without electricity or running water and wood heat. During those many years, they published 2 illustrated books of poetry together: *A Glimpse of Peace* and *Flickering Free*. Still in touch, *Why Not Love?* is their third collaboration.

In his own words: "I chose to ignore the world and never looked back. I can't align myself with much that's happening. There's so much going on in the world that still doesn't make any sense."

Ken Heitz has been a rustic furniture maker for 35 years.

Breinigsville, PA USA
06 July 2010
241212BV00001B/7/P